The History of
Permanence

The History of Permanence

GARY FINCKE

STEPHEN F. AUSTIN STATE UNIVERSITY PRESS
2011

Stephen F. Austin State University Press
P.O. Box 13007, SFA Station
Nacogdoches, TX   75962-3007
sfapress@sfasu.edu

Manufactured in the United States of America

LIBRARY OF CONGRESS IN PUBLICATION DATA
Fincke, Gary 1945-
The History of Permanence / Gary Fincke

p. cm.
ISBN: 978-1-936205-19-6

1. Poetry. 2. American Poetry. 3. Fincke, Gary.

The paper used in this book meets the requirements of ANSI/NISO Z39.48-1992
(R1997) (Permanence of Paper)

ACKNOWLEDGEMENTS

(some poems within the sequences have appeared in different form
individually)

"The Possibilities for Wings" *Virginia Quarterly Review*
"The Serious Surprise of Sorrow" *Alaska Quarterly Review*
"After the Aberfan Disaster" *The Gettysburg Review*
"The End of the World" *River Styx*
"The Dodo Exhibit" *Zoland Poetry Anthology*
"Learning to Stutter" *Margie*
"Eating the Clones" *Tar River Review*
"Meat Eaters" *Alaska Quarterly Review*
"In Theory" *Connotation Press*
"Selflessness" *Virginia Quarterly Review*
"The Dead Girls" *Ploughshares*
"Things that Fall from the Sky" *Beloit Poetry Journal*
"Something to Think About" Individually in *The Gettysburg Review,
Zoland Poetry Anthology, The Literary Review, Beloit Poetry Journal*
"The Etymology of Angels" *The Missouri Review*
"The Doctrine of Signatures" *Poetry Northwest*
"The Art of Moulage" *Ploughshares*
"Hanging the Pigs" *The Gettysburg Review*
"After the Crucifixion Act" *Night Train*
"Inevitability" *River Styx*
"Vestments" *Cold Mountain Review*
"Swarms" *The Literary Review*
"The Life Span of Honey" *Dos Passos Review*
"The History of Permanence" *Future Cycle*
ତ୍ର Individually in *Poetry Northwest, The North American Review,
The Laurel Review, Christian Century*
"You Know" *Harpur Palate*
"Specificity" *The Gettysburg Review*

CONTENTS

For Liz, Derek, Shannon, and Aaron
And in memory of Len Roberts

The Possibilites
For
Wings

The Possibilities for Wings

How often have the customs of strangers
Silenced me into dreaming their beliefs.
In Java, for example, some people
Insist the souls of suicides return
In the bodies of crows, while in Scotland,
Souls of the lonely flee to butterflies.

In Pennsylvania? In this town where death
Belongs to those with names I've said, the souls
Of the ordinary are cries called out
And gone into an afternoon of rain,
Leaving me to wish winged things for the friend
Whose heart has failed, the friend who killed himself
In his meticulously sealed garage.

In my back yard? I'm talking to the friend
Who, like me, has sidestepped the terrible,
And even, from time to time, laughs aloud,
Neither of us, not yet, fluttering off
In moths or whatever we might predict
For our futures, the possible wings for
Depression, jealousy, the waste of hours.

Choose one? he asks, and I say the poorwill,
The only bird that hibernates, waking,
After months, to flight. Yes, he answers, good.
Overhead, just now, a small plane pierces
The air, and I imagine both of us

On board, becoming birds that seem to fly
Without love of anything but ourselves,
Shaping our fear against the summoned sky.

The Serious Surprise of Sorrow

She's twelve, the girl who discovers a foot
Washed ashore in British Columbia.
Interviewed, she chatters, puzzled, amazed.

Attention is an awkward thing, she thinks,
And now she's been chosen as the witness
To the arrival of a miracle

Because two more feet, both left, like the one
She found, have landed on nearby beaches,
All of them wearing size 12 running shoes

Like a tiny cluster of rare cancer.
Surely they had mates, though left and right feet
Respond differently to the sea's currents,

According to the oceanographer
Who tracked, once, the paths of rubber ducks spilled
From a ship like a flotilla for joy.

Somewhere, then, the shoed right feet are floating
Toward another country, size 12 men
Targeted like unbribable judges.

Those feet will wash up on a thousand blogs;
Those feet will litter the crowded beaches
Of a million chat room conversations

Until time's incinerator turns them
To ash, becoming the urban legend
Of the wilderness that always concludes

With a girl who still believes that three men
Are limping somewhere on the prosthetics
For impossible chance, not already

Eaten by the grim mouths of the ocean,
That chosen girl growing into knowing
There is no limit to what we are asked

To accept, giving a personal name
To the serious surprise of sorrow,
Unable to stop scanning like those men

From our town's senior center who carry
Metal detectors to the nearby park,
Walking with stuttering steps like robins,

Their heads cocked a moment, then cocked again,
Their beaks passing over the unmown grass,
Listening for the soil's faintest sound.

After the Aberfan Disaster

On Oct. 21, 1966, in Wales, an 800 foot high "tip" of rock, coal,
mud, and shale collapsed, crushing an elementary school, killing 116
children and 5 teachers.

In this story, the assembled children
Have just sung "All Things Bright and Beautiful."
In this story, a survivor recalls
"In that silence you couldn't hear a bird,"
The slag thirty feet deep, a certainty.

In this story, the crushed children are called
By their parents. In this story, so few
Of them answer they become miracles,
The kind where ten lepers are cleansed, leaving
A colony of others to fester.

In this story, the children are smothered
By indifference, the company's and mine,
Because I am cowering from the draft,
Only college between me and combat.
That afternoon, I drive my father's car

One hundred miles per hour on a road
With a dozen intersections, and slow,
Trembling, into the sudden afterward
Of my brief, self-made miracle, thinking
What else proves I belong to the future?

Those children and their teachers are as dead
As two friends killed in cars. Some minister,
Days later, repeats, "In all things, design"
In a sermon I overhear, sounding
As if he's casting a blessing on rape.

A half mile from that service are slag heaps
High enough to take the light an hour
Early each evening. This story has me
Cautiously climbing each one with a friend
Soon to be blown apart in Vietnam.

Could there have been an alternate story
To the one I was breathing behind him?
So safely enrolled, who had I become
But a patient with purchased remission,
Reading about loss in expensive rooms?

The End of the World

Did you ever, as I did at six,
decide to walk to the world's end?
Me? I lasted two hours one morning
before I sat on a bench where
two strangers waited for a streetcar.
My hands turned busy with the cracks
in the painted wood. My fingernails,
right, then left handed, wrote my name
in the block letters I'd learned that year.
And because I wanted those men
to believe I was a special boy,
someone with loose change or tokens
in his pocket, so responsible
I could ride alone, I waited
like they did, posing as a rider.

When a car came, they boarded without
asking me about the blisters
that burned inside my shoes. The driver
stared forward and hissed shut the door.
In the corner of the shelter was
a robin covered with ants; near
the gray ceiling hung three spider webs,
and I understood that this was
where the world ended, that I needed
to turn around and haul that news
with me into the next day, throwing

away my blood-soaked socks, trusting
my mother not to notice one small
absence while I secretly soaked
my feet like I'd seen her do after
she finished a bakery day,
ten hours of standing and selling to
customers without mentioning
her corns and swollen veins, things she soaked,
saying they might vanish if she
could sit until the end of the world.

The Dodo Exhibit

The extinct elicit sympathy, birds
In particular, the large and flightless—
Great auks, elephant birds, the lost dodo,
All favorites of visitors who love
The museum's carefully mounted bodies.
Mostly, they show what islands do, allow
Anomalies until the world arrives
Like space men, the Rodrigues solitaire
One more absence, the dodo's close cousin
Vanished as well from its nearby island,
No one using its name as simile
Like my father, just now, remembering
"Dumb as a dodo" while he shuffles through
His erratic mind as if he's looking
For the seven of diamonds I once chose
When he taught an elementary trick,
Reversing the deck as I replaced it,
So simple a boy of seven could learn.
Instead, he shows me his leather necklace,
The dark cameo for emergency
That plays something like the awful squawking
From a flurry of frightened wings, the call
That will hurry the world to attend him.
He says he wears it for my sister's sake,
Letting her trust in the safety of sound.
"I'll die in my sleep," he says, the sentence
So clear among his daily confusions
I know he means to never press that sphere,

That he's dress-rehearsed his death already—
The heart attack detected, years later,
From its scarring; the fainting that ended
In a meadow, the car stalled, undamaged;
The private blackouts he's confessed like sins,
His heart hesitating, awkward, like birds
Gone fat and flightless into extinction,
Even those displayed a fabrication
Of chicken feathers, duck wings well-chosen,
The convincing, curled feathers of egrets.

Learning to Stutter

*In 1939, a group of normal-speaking orphans were labeled
as stutterers and studied for the effects of this label.*

About the experiment.
About the dissertation
that satisfied professors,
the room where orphans listened
to lessons that subtracted.
About that first-hand research,
the months of observation.
About the children who learned
to be verifications.
About approval. About
what's lost for the greater good.
About recrimination,
testimony that the tongue
can be crippled for words
to come, the stuttering lives.
About the longevity
of the collective lesson,
the terror of paragraphs.
About the lifelong recluse,
the chronically embarrassed.
About permanence, children
so expertly taught, they learned
an apprehension for sound.

About the church orphanage
I visited each summer,
the long tables for twenty,
the metal plates for food scraped
from enormous, steaming bowls.
About the boy who stuttered
and the one who never spoke,
staying inside silence where
his sentences were perfect.
About fear's darkening smirk,
the blue going black of speech.
About me stuttering for
two days, learning to be cruel.
About my mother saying
I'd be unable to stop,
that I'd learn to be crippled.
About the defects in boys
she pointed out, their mumbling,
their slang, and their sentences
full of double negatives,
close cousins to stuttering.
About how I'd be like them,
like everybody else, weak.

Eating the Clones

FDA says clones' offspring may be in food supply

At the clone farm, the goats expect food;
The pigs are indifferent as we try
To pick out the parents among them.
We follow the invisible fence
While two mixed-breed dogs, on our side, bark
Furiously at the skittish hooves.
Some memorable red meat is about
To reach our plates again, a strip steak
So familiar it's almost friendly.
Such perpetuity is one kind
Of heaven we love to imagine,
Like believers in previous lives,
Dating our endings through centuries,
Including deaths by drowning, dagger,
And a rope pulled tight around the throat.
Willing, even, to be child victims
Because they're always resurrected.

So many ways we're eaten, we have
To anticipate our future selves,
Sitting up at night with memories
Unaccounted for, our past bodies
So nearly seen they seem like portraits.
Now, at the end of generations,
Families will be formed like puddles
From a neglected hose, the children
Splashing from one stain to the other

As if they were flat stones for fording.
Windows will be empty of mothers,
Their words become moths fluttering up
From flour and rice and shelves of spices,
Dry goods' spontaneous miracles.
Before chewing, we will dip our bread
In the thin au jus of the future,
And then the lifting of knives and forks,
Becoming what we've already been.

Meat-Eaters

In B-films, the carnivorous plants
Are always huge. They swallow anyone
Who wanders near, a single knot of vines

Tugging a victim into the dark maw
Of horror, not discriminating
At all, as if eating were accident,

As if they were human. The real killers?
Some work together like the field
Of sundews, in England, that ate,

Within hours, millions of butterflies,
One true story that illustrates
The collective achievement of plants.

But working alone, selectivity
Is what matters. The Venus flytrap
Measures its meals so it doesn't

Squander the down time of digestion
Upon the undersized. The jaw seals
Slowly, the spaces between its teeth

Allowing the escape of small insects.
So size-selective, its mouth, the young
Can flee, the tiny can skitter away,

Not through mercy, but efficiency,
What's necessary for survival
When rooted in the earth's poorest soil.

In Theory

A cosmological bomb billions of times more powerful than the atomic bomb might be created.

Luis Sancho, cosmologist

From one chance in ten to one in fifty,
The odds one scientist offers, speaking
Like a bookie about the end of Earth
When the new superconductor begins
To operate at full power next year.

A fool's bet, doubling down on prophecy,
But there's been lower odds and we're still here,
The world at DefCon 2, planes in the air,
Silos poised, those simultaneous keys
Locked and loaded, once, near our neighborhoods.

It's exaggeration, right? That work-stop
Injunction will be dismissed when colleagues
Set the odds at state-lottery levels,
Ready to be romantic, approaching
The speed of light, cozying up so tight
To the Big Bang, first cousin to the gods.

Chain reactions? That news arrives on canes,
Old as mutual assured destruction.
Now, showers of heavy-mass particles
Might end us with ultra-dense quark matter.
Now, the vocabulary for theory
Is elastic, stretching like bright pink gum
On the fingers of a delighted child.

And yet, this week, after friends my age died
On successive days, I woke on the third
To a phone call I believed was one more,
As if a chain reaction had begun
The way it did when one molested boy,
Last month, testified, toppling the next boy
And the next and the next into four days
Of soft, public confession, creating
The calendar of a local man's lust
On a Snyder County courtroom transcript.

And whether, at last, the seven billion
Of us become fodder for a black hole,
The wonder remains, those men and women
Waiting for the first light of computers
To show the hail of the hypothesized,
The high-speed pilgrimage to origin.
In theory. In trained imagination.
For they are on the brink of Genesis,
Hurtling back to the sea, forgetting air,
Sex, and the first impossible splitting
Until nothing is alive but the gods.

Selflessness

In the animal kingdom, among fish,
one father carries all of the laid eggs
in his mouth, sixty-five day starvation
to make that flexible, deep mouth a womb.

Such sacrifice, spitting them out at last,
following that fast with the daily chores
of parenting: to guard them while they feed,
to take them back into his mouth like God.

Those babies need to grow before something
hungry finds them. They need a place to sleep
safe enough to wake again to feeding,
watched carefully by their selfless father.

He's a living prayer, that catfish who knows
each child as he opens his mouth for them.
Though every father has limits, and so
does this one, turning his back, one morning,

as they feed, swimming away while he still
knows them, before his children grow so large
he can't tell them from what he hungers for.
If he forgets to flee, he will eat them.

The Dead Girls

The Dead Girls

1

The girl who martyred her dolls, sending them
To heaven to wait for her arrival,
Sentenced them to stones or fire or the force
Of her hands to tear them, methods she'd learned
From the serious, dark nuns who taught her.

She would press a pillow over my face
To encourage sainthood. "Now," she would say,
Leaning down, and I'd let myself go limp
And lie quietly for her arrangements.

Her hands clasped like Mary's in the painting
Over her bed, she prayed for my body.
Sparingly, she sprinkled me with lotion.
Always, because she'd taught the proper way
To stare, my eyes were open when I died.

That summer, in the months before fourth grade,
Her uniforms waited in the closet
For September, her white communion dress
Beside them, declaring to St. Agnes,
Who watched from the sunlit, opposite wall.

In August, her mother ran a vacuum
Through the house, moving from the living room
Of St. Francis to the narrow hallway
Of Our Lady of Lourdes, and I stayed dead

Until the sound reached that girl's room, rising
To her mother's clenched roar of cleanliness,
Both of us keeping our feet off the floor,
Giving her a swipe of room to work, clearing
The way for temporary perfection.

2

The girl who loved to be touched in cemeteries,
Who said the dead reminded her to ecstasy,
Offered her body to my hands while I agreed,
Thanking the lost for their shadowed grove of headstones.

Always it was dark or nearly so, that girl shy
About her disrespect or nakedness, until,
At last, approaching cemeteries in weak light
Made me want to fuck above a thousand strangers.

One night, accidentally, the death of someone
Both of us knew, someone our age, meaning nineteen.
The violence of loss a lump underneath us
No matter which well-tended garden we entered.

Though frankly, we were exhausted by then, tired
Of each other's needs, and the dead could do nothing
Except talk among themselves about our absence,
Using the inaudible language of the earth.

3

The girl who died the following day
Is still talking in my car. She sits

Beside me, knees drawn up to her chin
Like a pouting child. Expectation
Is the only thing that will happen
Between us, the car's radio full
Of the British Invasion until
I follow her under the driveway's
Double floodlights to the house I will
Never be inside. "Next week," she says,
Before I drive past where she will die
In another boy's new car, the site
So often seen I notice nothing
But oncoming headlights, the bright ones
Under the influence of midnight,
The day she will die just now begun,
The radio switched to Marvin Gaye
And James Brown, the road so familiar
I can be careless with attention
As I speed toward the unexpected,
What weekends are for, story makers.

Things that Fall
from the Sky

Things that Fall from the Sky
(A Sequence)

Seeds

Take one early evening. A father calls
His wife and children outside to witness
The eastern sky going bloody with clouds.
"What?" they say, transfixed, "What?" staring skyward
Until the rain swarms like sand, a brief storm
Of seeds that spreads them apart, their eyes closed
Under this brief anomaly of hail.

The after-light is so yellow it seems
To have traveled here from a jaundiced star.
Before he can speak, the father must kneel
To examine that rain, his wonder turned
Watery, doubt taking his fingertips
Over their pinpricked skin to read the Braille
Of what might be born from a vocal rain.

A name for the first day of invasion
Wells up in him, a long vowel that leaves
Its breath on their faces. When they watch him
Like babies, that man smiles the first falsehood
Of devotion, afraid they already
Believe so much in these seeds, they'll swallow,
Certain that superstition will feed them.

Powder

*In 1969, in South Carolina, nondairy creamer from the new
Borden plant began to fall on a small town.*

1

The day became white and sweet
Like the air above a rolling pin

As a woman thins the dough
For chip-filled cookies. Children stood

Beside their mothers, their hands
Clutching toys they would not part with.

2

The weather cut the neighborhood
Into the shapes of families.

The cloud was soluble on tongues.
It surrounded each face like sound.

Already there were footprints
On sidewalks, a dream of shovels.

3

Those dusted by light took vows.
Suddenly, declarations of love,

The streets become hospitals.
Time was ending. A memory

Of old prophecies collected
In the eyes of everyone.

4

At last, the company's reassurance,
Though later, when the whitened bathed,

They stroked the film that had formed
Along their cheeks, their fingertips

Dizzy with the wonder of children
Touching the rouged faces of the dead.

Documents

*In 1973 a set of papers that explained, with graphs and
formulas, "normalized extinction" and the Davis-Greenstein
mechanism of astrophysics, fell from a distance higher than a
300-foot radio transmission tower.*

When the paper fell from the sky, it looked
As if a briefcase had opened, a latch
Sprung loose among the clouds, spilling a set
Of documents, nothing in that story
To rush cameras right over, not when
There'd been a robbery and a fire, not when
The news desk smelled the late night stink of hoax.

But there was the detail of the tower,
How its height was cited, and documents
Aren't a rock format prank. Moreover,
This caller worked in radio, a sort
Of cousin to humor when he described
Formulas and graphs, suggesting a plot

Filled with spies or scientists dangerous
With political or religious hate.
A few lines then. A small item below
An ad for dishwashers, television
Running a gutted house and empty safe
As if its news were in summer reruns.
But after, when no one claimed those papers,
Chosen repeated itself like *amen*
As the last word of that witness' thoughts.

Prophecy, now, was physics, difficult
As a burning bush or exploding star.
And didn't "normalized extinction" sound
Like a careless spin on nuclear war?
He remembered the meteor legend,
How it explained the end of dinosaurs,
All things large starving in the dusty years
Of toxic darkness. Scholarship set in
Like the deep winter of apprehension.
Each night, before looking up, he wished for
The empty sky of the ordinary.

Meat

After meat fell from the sky,
After that shower ended
Like a cold tap twisted shut,
There were men who sampled it,
Cautiously chewing like kings.
Like mutton, one said, relieved,
Or venison, second choice,

Someone suggesting vultures
Had vomited together
From overhead; somebody,
At last, saying they were scraps
From God's table, calling up
The old words for mystery
That caught in the throat like bones.
The men who had eaten coughed
While wishes circulated
Like secrets pledged to silence.
For days, children examined
Their fathers for fur and claws.
Old wives were as tentative as
The child brides they had been, deep
In the nineteenth century
When transubstantiation
Was a bright, beautiful fact.

So it is with the strange.
A choir of analysts
Performed the old cantata
Of certainties until meat
Was people who had been ripped
To pieces by the sharp scythe
Of tornado, their parts swirled
Upward and returned as rain.
A family was missing.
Parables were passed through yards
Until streets of disciples
Formed a holy neighborhood.
A chattering of voices
Settled on porches, the words

So much the same they sounded
Like clouds of starlings rising.

Bodies

Begin with the one that famously
Landed on a San Diego car,
Dropping from a mid-air accident
Like a fantastically narrow storm.
Nothing can come from such plummeting
But disaster or the miracle
That needs snow drifts and touch downs precise
As ones that land softly on Mars, yet
The melodrama transfixes us
The way children, once, at matinees,
Were caught by serial cliffhangers
And spent a week believing rescue
As impossible as growing old.

That driver and her child were unharmed,
But afterward, she had a habit
Of glancing up like a forecaster,
Though it's rare, anyone looking up
For the descent of bodies, rarer
To believe they're falling from a cloud.
It takes the height that turns us breathless,
A thousand feet or more to make us
Think "sky" like one morning when distance
Throttled our breath while suited bodies
Plunged like drops of a passing shower

That pockmark the dust of current drought.

And I, for once, agreed on something
With my sad, conservative neighbors,
Desiring a sect of people dead,
Their lives snuffed by gene anomaly.
The body of Christ, the blood of Christ—
The chorus of communion became
The password into our side for war.
It drummed in the inner ear like pulse,
And I dreamed myself marching to plant
The first flag of a lifetime, tending
It each morning as if cloth might die
And declare me criminal and cruel
In the common carelessness of peace.

Something to Think About

Something to Think About
(a sequence)

It's Something

Who isn't taken by stories like the one
About M. Boulard, who owned seven houses,
Each of them bearing a hundred thousand books.
Or Richard Heber, who believed he needed
Three copies of every volume, eight houses
In three countries necessary to hold them.

And reading those numbers, who doesn't decide
There's likely no limit for hoarders, someone
Like Sir Thomas Phillips, who wanted the most,
Driving two wives crazy with his collection,
Intending to own every book in the world.

And lately, my neighbor, not mentioned, not yet,
In such lists, though he buys books by the thousands,
Clearing out sales from garages and front yards
To fill his basement floor to ceiling, starting,
This year, on rooms left vacant by his daughters
Grown and gone, arranging his hundred thousand
In chronological order to create,
He says, the twentieth century of books,
Including seven copies of *Blue Highways*
And six of *Road Song*, the doubles and triples
He shows me when I follow his guided tour.

Downstairs, I imagine fire; upstairs, collapse,
His house imploded by millions of pages.
I stand beside him in his daughter's bedroom,
The 90s surrounding us, and think of books
I've published, none visible upon these shelves.
Next door is the 80s, the odds long against
My earliest, and I remember searching
Bookstore shelves, drifting down the Fs, despondent.

I keep to myself that I own seventy
Of one title, thirty-five of another,
Lugging them to readings where they leak away,
Some evenings, one by one. My neighbor, standing
Where his house is clear, sweeps his large hands apart
As if he's showing me stars, the infinite
Sprawled and demanding to be seen. A second,
Then two, he holds them wide until I manage,
"It's something," backing into the driveway where
His station wagon sits low and stacked, waiting
Like a boxcar for his insatiable hands.

Weighing the World

*Dying, Henry Cavendish, the reclusive scientist, ordered his
servants from the room because he had "something to think about."*

Begin with Cavendish proving that water
Wasn't the element the world thought it was.
Follow that with his silence, how frightening
All women were, so unbearable to glimpse
He left notes for his housekeeper, constructing

A second staircase for her exclusive use.

Such seclusion is its own education,
The bookishness of silence teaching, subject
By subject, what haunts sufficiently to say.
An example? Cavendish, so mute, would weigh
The world by calculating its density,
Sending his proof to ordinary people
Who had learned the density of feigned friendships,
To weigh anger, disinterest, and disdain.

Now imagine Cavendish, one afternoon,
Paused at the base of the housekeeper's staircase,
That woman on errands he's put in writing.
Certain of her absence, he begins to climb,
Reaches the second floor to stand on a spot
So strange he hears the light in a foreign tongue.
Then think of the scenario for descent,
The choice, if he lingers, of her stairs or his.

Improbable? Once, during a reception,
I spent an hour alone in an upstairs room
Where I'd carried two glasses of chardonnay
Like a husband. There were books and photographs,
A bed perfectly made by the housekeeper
My university gives its president.

I sat on the one shadowed chair where his wife
Would examine herself, perhaps, before sleep,
The house beneath me so dense with my colleagues
It grew gravity that kept me from rising.
Eleven sets of footsteps passed in the hall;

Each time a toilet flushed and water ran
Before they reversed direction like sentries.
Sitting there, I had something to think about,
How all those guests would honor the promises
They'd spoken to leave solitude to others.
At last, I calculated the weight of lies
I needed to carry downstairs. I finished
That wine and placed both glasses on the table
Beside the hardbound stories of Henry James.

Regaining my feet was as hard as rising
After a week of flu. *There,* I thought, *like that,*
Hand on the polished railing and then, three steps
From the foot of the stairs, letting go, prepared.

Competitive Eating

Famously, this summer, sixty-eight hot dogs,
Buns included, were swallowed in twelve minutes
At Coney Island, the beach packed with people
Transfixed by that brief, marvelous appetite.

Wonders, for sure, those numbers and the workings
Of the body to accept them, a strangeness
Like the swords and fire down the throats at sideshows,
But now there's an alphabetical roster

Of records for quantity and speed, starting
With asparagus, six pounds in ten minutes,
Followed by beef tongue, bologna, burritos,
The beautiful simplicity of buffet.

Alliterations of the edible fill
The page: cabbage and candy, connoli, corn,
And the connotative mention of cow brains,
Fifty-seven of them in fifteen minutes

By the same phenom who Hoovered those hot dogs.
Matzo balls, mayonnaise, meat pies—suddenly,
The weight of eating mesmerizes like breasts,
And I remember my single fling with food,

Choosing goldfish, live ones, and betting with friends
Before taking them down with water to win
Ten dollars for a dozen in a minute,
My unrecorded record for childishness.

Look, there are mouths for stones and metal and glass,
Things to be more careful with than tamales,
No limit to what we're willing to swallow—
Paragraphs of protest, a declaration

Of love, promises, dreams. Ceaselessly, we can
Listen for our sentences washed back with spit.
If we stay quiet, holding our breath, we might
Hear the infinity of words within us.

Steinmetz in the Canoe

Where he loved to work, using
A desk of boards, an office
Engineered for drifting

On a man-made pond.
So why shouldn't Steinmetz look
Satisfied, even healthy,
Not crippled like he appears
In that famous photograph
With Einstein, who stands taller
And straighter and better dressed
Than Steinmetz, who all but falls
Sideways while the camera
Catches his hunchback.
It was General Electric
That sold this version of their star,
Steinmetz dwarfed by
The Nobel Laureate, and nothing now
Can undo that deep shadow,
Not even the admission,
Later, that the photograph
Is altered, that they were posed,
That day, among twenty men,
That Steinmetz, too, would doctor
Photos, placing his image
In boats with young, beautiful
Women, cloning himself, each
Couple floating on water,
Perfectly paired electrons.

The Prophecies of Mathematics

Not even his wife wanted to listen
To Francis Galton explain that prayer made
No difference, that insurance companies

Knew the facts of longevity, and there
Was no adjustment for people who prayed
And the various buildings they lived in.
Not even, but he said it anyway—
The pious live no longer than the bad.
It's always this way with Jeremiahs.
In the prophecies of mathematics
Are equations for hours in the sun,
Alcohol in the blood, early marriage.
There, among the numbers, lies the total
Of the truth of ourselves, and I admit
I've counted the daily steps from my house
To my office through six possible routes;
I've counted the frequency of letters,
Rooting for underdogs like b and k
To outdo their predicted sums of use.

Trivial? Stupid? I estimated
The minutes, once, until the end of school,
Wrote seventy-five thousand, six hundred,
In my September notebook and followed
The lurch of each long minute on the clock
For three periods of world history,
Latin, and plane geometry until
I rejoined the classroom of common sense,
Abandoning the women who number
The knocks on a door to seven, the breaths
Before starting their cars to six, knowing
Nothing about the habits of Galton,
Who kept track of boredom by numbering
The small fidgets of a congregation,

Who counted the brush strokes as his portrait
Was painted, who evaluated place,
At last, by the beauty of its women,
Selecting London like a pageant judge,
Leaving it to us to tally the days
Till what's longed for may or may not arrive,
Keeping calendars of Xs that end,
Each time, on the eve of possible joy
Like a merciless cliffhanger for faith.

Hypergraphia

*During World War II, Geoffrey Pyke designed an "ice battleship"
that would have been 2000 feet long and weigh 2,200,000 tons*

Early in a paperback on genius,
The chapter about the unrecognized,
Geoffrey Pyke makes ice indestructible
By adding perfect amounts of wood pulp.
For battleships, he says. For victory.
And proven, his wartime idea floats,
Unused, while conventional fleets succeed.
Years of this, the unrealized, proposing
To the skeptical, each day statistics
And silenced projections, writing until,
With all that time saved by working in bed,
Not wasting hours of rising and dressing,
He proves the insomnia of despair.
His last night, for once clean-shaven, he looks
As ordinary as the generals
Who half-listened. He swallows pills and writes.

He empties a bottle and keeps writing,
Furious with final words while they turn
As illegible as the last sentence
In my A-student's suicide blue book.
Her detail of pills. Her apology.
"I don't want a scene," she wrote, flinging me
Down the sunlit hall to save her, nothing
Like my mother's clear script the day she died,
Writing, "I've never felt so nauseous,"
Fearing her kidneys failed. And after that?
Not a word about prayer, her remedy
For sin and sickness and disappointment.
She wrote about the bowl game my father
Was watching because Pittsburgh was playing.
She wrote a paragraph about Christmas,
A sentence about her fatigue and pain.
She must have made my father, at half time,
Walk that one-page letter to the mailbox
And flag it for delivery because
It lay among tax forms and catalogues
When I returned, after her funeral,
To open a week of mail, her mercy
Of words introducing eternity.

Ferris

For sure, there were worries—
That the wheel wouldn't turn,
That terrible weather
Would topple that thing or
Passengers uproot it

By shifting to one side.
So when summer's worst storm
Approached, Ferris gathered
His wife into the wind,
Rotating up, assured
As angels while the rest
Of Chicago rode
With the reporter
Who needed to prove
A city to the storm,
Lifting into the sky
Like a disciple
Of the machine age,
Ascending into
The windswept chill
Of survival, recording
That astonishing circle
Like a new testament,
Speaking the buoyant
Language of re-entry.

Sticktoitiveness

*Edward Leedskalnin, behind a wall and by himself,
constructed an allegorical temple from hard coral in South
Florida.*

What do we want, tourists at strange sites
Like Leedskalnin's coral furniture
Within and without his house of stone?

Here is the rock home for the three bears,
Goldilocks-guests testing beds and chairs,
Believing, for now, in the porridge
Of a stranger's imagination.
Here, the first secret is work alone;
The second, persistence, all of us
Waking to impossible bodies
Of our own, the ones, if they last, that
Will spend years untouched, moving about
Like stone, heavy and hard, dependent
On the obligations of others.
Sticktoitiveness—my father's language,
Meaning school and jobs and living a life
Of faith, citing Gutzon Borglum's long haul
On Mt. Rushmore, Korczak Ziolkowski's
Decades on the unfinished Crazy Horse,
Following forty years of labor
Through a series of photos, selecting
A stone from the pile of rubble offered
As souvenirs to tourists who marveled
And returned to their own endless tasks.

Sticktoitiveness—I've flown to China,
A place for which he has no reference.
I tell him what I've witnessed from a bus,
The collective discipline of thousands
Of men rebuilding a highway by hand,
The guide assuring our group those workers
Would finish in several years, leaving
The number to us as some of those men
Hauled stones in wheelbarrows, some wielded picks
Or leaned into spades, the broken road lined

With makeshift homes surrounded by women
And children who followed their work, putting
The paved behind them like a monument,
Moving this perseverance by the mile.

Sticktoitiveness—my father tells me
The tale of Alan Foresman, who labored
On a letter to his wife for two years,
Using more than a million words to write
That novel of thoughts. Sticktoitiveness—
Year by year, I have given my father
All of my twenty-one books, expecting
Something, receiving, in exchange, "What's next?"
As if I were Yuan K'ai, the monk who carved
A two hundred foot Buddha out of rock,
Working seventy years, working alone.

The Etymology
of
Angels

The Etymology of Angels

In Beloit, Wisconsin, a woman answers
The door in wings and halo, silver dress,
Welcomes me to her ten thousand angels
With "take your time and enjoy," fluttering
Like the authors of books who promise
Winged guardians are keeping us from harm.
The angel of the good deed, the angel
Of the safety net—half who answer polls
Believe, anxious as hospice visitors
Who avoid the terrible use of *next*.
Here is the theory of the angels who
Started a pilot program to transform
The world, two hundred fifty years renewed
Like a government grant. Here is the woman
Who encourages us to relax into
Our "sacred space" and wait for personal
Messages from heaven. Here is the handbook
For aspiring angels, how to provide,
How to facilitate, how to answer
The phone for the great CEO and transmit
The celestial e-mail to the faithful.
In the etymology of angels,
Diminishment sticks like a persistent gene
Until they sparkle like ten thousand pieces
Of kitsch, a woman's dress, the gaze of Azrail
Staring from the upstairs window as I leave,
One of his six billion eyes fixed on me.

And all along the rain swept interstate,
From the passenger side of each car that
Hisses by, Azrail mouthing the census
With one of his six billion tongues, adding
And subtracting while I form six billion
Questions of my own for the earnest angel
Who folds her pale hands, leans forward with knees
Together. This interview starts with Where
And When and Why, and this personal angel,
So professional, asks me to answer these
Myself because she's been employed and trained
By the great deflector, or perhaps that's what
Matters or else nothing matters at all.

The Doctrine of Signatures

The woman who followed me from flower
To flower said Birthday? Anniversary?
And I shook my head among the arrangements
Until she shifted to Accident? Sickness?
Guiding and pointing and introducing
The Doctrine of Signatures, how all plants
Were created to serve us, their powers
To cure revealed by shape, by size, by shade:
The bloodshot blossoms of the eyebright
Heal pinkeye; the Chines lantern plant
Is bladder-shaped for stones. Paracelsus,
She said, acknowledging her source, adding
Yellow plants for the liver, ginseng root
For general malaise, prescriptions
So simple we could arrange eternity
In a greenhouse if we knew the shapes
Of our weakest parts, my mother's heart
Winding down while I thought of petals
Red and sugared as a lover's gift.
And since then I've comparison-shopped
For pancreas, thyroid, lymph glands, walking
The aisles with such ignorance of form
I might as well choose a shape for the soul—
Lilac, lily, morning glory—as if
Resurrection could be watered and fed
While we search for the flowers that form
Like tumors, the buds that open into

The ominous mass on the x-ray,
And the seeds or spores that are scattered
Like great seasonings for the earth, blended
So perfectly they lie invisible
Until they rise form our astonished tongues.

The Art of Moulage

For dermatology, for the betterment
Of medical science, Joseph Towne produced
Over five hundred models of skin disease,
Forming those faces from beeswax and resin,
Applying disease with spatulas and knives--
Lesions and rashes, pustules, and the chancres
Of unchecked syphilis, especially those
On faces disfigured by heredity,
Bad luck, or unwisely satiated lust.

An art, getting sickness just right, and there were
Others, like Jules Baretta, who created
Two thousand moulages, some of which followed
The changes in flesh from first symptom to death.
What's necessary to warn us? Tumors? Wounds?
Neither of those masters would share the secrets
Of his work, refusing to teach the darkness
Of gangrene, the inflammation where it spreads.

My father, near ninety, declares his creased face
Unrecognizable. My friend's mother, whose
Beautiful face was shredded through a windshield,
Lifts her right hand to the dense thicket of scars
When someone approaches. . . Look, an hour ago,
The harelips splitting the faces of children
Made me turn a page of a news magazine,
Sending me back to the soft community
Of the unscarred that turns away, revolted,

From the terrible commonplace of acne
And shingles; from warts, boils, melanoma—
And yet, with models, we are fascinated
By the possibilities of the body,
What we are capable of turning into,
Misery thriving until our skin becomes
A sieve for horror that rises through the pores.

Hanging the Pigs

*During the Middle Ages, there were dozens
of murder trials against animals.*

For murder, it was always
The domesticated, pigs
Especially, the ones who
Trampled children, danced their hooves
Through memory's red seizure.

The pigs, sometimes, were tortured,
Squealed clear confessions of guilt.
And locked in solitary,
They grunted the black mass prayer,
Snuffled to the devil's sleep,
So closely guarded, so bound,
None of those killers escaped.

And when they trotted, back-whipped,
To trial, a few of those pigs,
According to the records,
Had court-appointed lawyers
To plead the victim-defense,
The mental-deficiency
Gambit, none of it moving
The men who stood in for God.

So all were executed.
Hammered. Butchered. Some led
To the gallows, snouts sliced off,
Wearing white human masks, dressed

In coats and trousers, lifted
To the bleating, back-legged stance
Of the hell-Pentecost, all
The silenced crowd pressed forward,
Waiting for those pigs to hang,
Shutting up their Satan tongues.

After the Crucifixion Act

Jesus, I begin, you already know
The secrets of re-enactment, the holes
Well-placed in the hands kept open with pegs,
Much like wearing gold through the ears and nose.
You know the history of its illusion,
Including Tommy Minnock, famously
Singing "After the Ball is Over" while
Nailed to a cross, and Mortado, who hid
Blood packs in his permanent stigmata.

Jesus, I confess to re-enactment,
Waking before sunrise to stand in snow
To see my shadow stretch into forecast.
I've driven to Kent State, in early May,
To stand in the spaces where classmates died.
I've played annual martyr for nothing
But rage at anyone in uniform.
Last week, at Gettysburg, the costumed blue
And gray marched in the early July heat,
And I met three Confederates who smoked
Behind a bar, drunk enough to believe
I wanted to hear each place they'd been shot
That afternoon, one dying ten steps short
Of Cemetery Ridge. "Right here," he said,
Pointing to his chest, and I thought he might
Open his nineteenth-century shirt to
A scar like my father lately come down
From the cross of surgery, heart restored,

Singing his own hymn to resurrection,
Telling me, "Touch it," and pressing my hand
To the raised evidence of miracle.

Jesus, you already know someone, once,
Suffered nails driven through his unmarked hands
And feet, forcing his audience to flee.
You already know it's the illusion
We want, the crucified returning for
Curtain calls, smiling and accepting praise.
Don't we wound enough with the hammered spikes
Of love? This summer a neighbor kidnapped
His former wife from the hospital where
She worked and fucked her on his van's back seat
Before shooting her. He pointed the gun
At his head and pantomimed suicide
Until he rolled aside the van's blue door
And surrendered himself to the future.
And now I can't stop following these words
To something worse than paid-for blasphemy,
Re-enacting the hell of history.

The Woman Who Used Snakes as a Weapon

Some nights disturbing the peace can turn serious,
The argument jacked up by drugs or alcohol
To runway volume while it looks for loaded guns.
Jealousy. Despair. The police, at last, arrive,
And confrontation follows like an untrained dog.

One such evening, a woman too loud for neighbors
Owned snakes, and she used them, hissing "Back off," lifting
The copperheads, two per steady hand, to brandish
Like an automatic weapon, defense enough
To earn an hour of curses in a cop-filled room.

She had the faith of those churchgoers who decide
The saved by their ease with snake handling, but her pets
Were leery of the small congregation of law.
They sensed, right off, that religion wasn't a force
In that room, that blasphemy was self-defeating.

So she was bitten, and more than once, disarming
Herself by dropping those serpents back under glass.
It wasn't surrender, she said, this giving in.
Just a truce, like in the old stories of soldiers
She'd read about, the ones who climbed out of trenches

To celebrate Christmas Eve with the enemy.
I know my poisons, she said. I can still be saved.

The police were listening as if they'd shot her.
Even with her reduced to patient, they kept space
Between them and her, overheard their beating hearts.

Miss Hartung Teaches Us One Way to Die

Listen now, in Boston, once, in January,
The brief, false promise of spring pushed people outside
Just when a huge tank of molasses burst open
Like the Johnstown Dam. Think of that, children, a wave
As high as a house coming down Commercial Street.
It's a miracle only twenty-one were drowned,
Though nothing, Miss Hartung said, is impossible.

And why would anybody, you're all asking, store
Two million gallons? Do your fathers favor rum?
Consider this. The rest of Boston, curious,
Walked through molasses to see how others could die.
They carried goop on their shoes for miles, took the smell
Of sweetness back home with them like second-hand smoke.
For weeks they talked about nothing but molasses.

Don't laugh. There's always an excess that wants let loose.
For example, what are your bedrooms downhill from?
Each and every one of you live below something,
Even if it's simply a cloudless, benign sky.

Inevitability

*There are degrees of damage, from regional devastation to
global catastrophe, which happens every 100,000 years or less—*
from THE TORINO SCALE

Call it the salt of judgment, somebody
Adding "of course" to stories like this one
About Tom Chapman dying in a crash,
Lucky to last this long, driving twelve years
With hand controls after he'd lost his legs
In a high-speed, all night drinking, head-on.

Me? I remembered the Torino Scale,
Which sets the odds for debris striking us
From space, the risk code from 0 to 10
In bands of white, yellow, orange and red
As if meteors were the dirty bombs
Of extraterrestrial terrorists.

Not that I didn't agree, listening
To myself for an hour as I pedaled
A bicycle and calibrated ways
To be ended--heart attack, accident,
Cancer and stroke, the most likely methods
To strike me before the morning ended.

But driving home, I remembered the year
I was a passenger a dozen times
In Tom Chapman's red Thunderbird, each trip
Thinking of my face thrown through the windshield,
My body hurled into a tree or pole
Or the miraculous meadow of safe.

And one afternoon, when we'd swallowed beer
Into the idea of being blond,
We soaked our hair in bleach and sunned ourselves
To streaks of gold and orange, luminous
With love for ourselves before Chapman said,
"Of course" when I wouldn't get in his car.

A good call, that refusal. He lasted
Three miles before he struck a tree, rolling
Into explosion he was thrown clear of,
Sending me sober to each seat I took
Behind the wheel where I lowered my speed
And believed myself safe as a planet

Whose odds of destruction are classified
"Below random," "random," "most unlikely,"
Those categories of reassurance
Changed, by colors, to "meriting concern,"
"Significant threat," and the brilliant red
Of "the certain global catastrophe."

And I nod, right now, fundamentalist
For risk, inevitability's code
Running to ten on the Torino Scale
For the body, knowing Tom Chapman slammed
A pale, concrete pillar beneath a bridge,
Repeating "of course" like the self-righteous,

And returning to where Tom Chapman, once,
Walked away from both injury and death.
The tree, forty years later, stands like stone,
Beating the steep odds of it being there,

Surviving disease and developers
And whatever anger I bring with me,

Staring, finally, at the sky, as if
I could pick out the code-red asteroid
Or guess which star has been dark for decades,
Even as it dazzles like the millions
Still burning, even as I bet my choice
At the prohibitive odds for heaven.

Vestments

Once, a boy was carried from church
under the arm of his father.
The last six pews of worshipers
saw him kick and flail, including
another boy his age who stared
as if he were a netted fish.
That father took him to the room
where vestments were kept, the colors
arranged in stacks for each season
of God and Christ. A surplice hung
as carefully as a bride's dress;
the father said, "You sit right here
until you start acting your age."
When the boy wailed, he said, "If you
die right now, you'll go straight to hell."

That boy was five, less than a month
from beginning school, and after
his father locked him in, he held
his breath and listened for the scrape
of devils' claws underneath him.
His father, outside, counted to
three hundred, long enough, he thought,
for a lesson, and he opened
the door to see his son wearing
the minister's green stole, sitting
in that chair, head down and staring

where a centipede was crawling,
unaware in the light, the boy
unmoving as a murdered child,
the gold fringe of the stole almost
touching the polished floor, the cross
and crown near each end wavering
from the first terror of belief.

Swarms

*The Parasitoid wasp can survive more than four times
the radiation than a roach can.*

One morning, my wife called to warn me that
Roaches were swarming in the living room.
She whispered as if they were listening.

For sixty years now, the myth of roaches,
Its prophecy resting in the bellies
Of airplanes and silos, inside the holds
Of submarines ceaselessly circling while
We've memorized the extinction details
Of vomit and lost hair, of lives banished
From a planet of insects that scurry
In the dark, waking nobody from sleep.

One afternoon, my daughter, eight years old,
Memorized the definition of *swarm*
As she flailed at a thick flurry of wasps.

How we've shuddered reading Revelation
In the Postmodern Testament, but now
We learn that promise won't be kept, that when
Radiation saturates air and earth
And water, when everything is poisoned,
Roaches vanished, just these wasps will survive
The way this new Jeremiah of war
Has foretold the world with us, a hell
Of crawling replaced by a hell of flight.
One evening, *swarm* shuddered up within me

For ants at our sidewalk cracks, for fruit flies
Surrounding our trash, for caterpillars
Incubating inside translucent tents
On our blossoming decorative trees,
Any of those gatherings sufficient
To terrorize with their numbers, the way,
In crowded foreign cities, the jabber
Of a language we do not understand
Becomes a buzz or a drone or even,
The definitive sound of the future.

The Life Span of Honey

Hard and problematic, six years untouched
In the darkness of a contested will,
Four children coming to carry away
Their tiny wants, then not coming at all
Until the windows are broken by boys,
The cupboards of the woman who died here
Opened by the couple who used her bed.

Now, that woman occupies every room.
She crowds the kitchen with seventy years
Of voice that passes for wind as they find,
In a Mason jar, the honey that lived
With that woman for a third of her life,
Opened and closed and finally reset
On the pantry shelf for things not needed.

Forever fresh, the label says, as if
The dead might reacquire the old desire
For sweetness, that woman they did not know
Pushing up from her chair with toasted bread.
Just below that crystal rind, honey waits
Unspoiled, outlasting litigation,
The dark, protracted arguments of grudge.

And there, before arson, a boy stirs it
With one finger to test his lover's trust.
And when she extends her tongue, eyes open,
He lays thick drops upon it, loving her

As she swallows, her dress already down,
The beauty of her breasts so luminous
He's afraid his hands might pass right through her.

The History of
Permanence

The History of Permanence
(a sequence)

Learning the Lifespan

Methuselah, the Genesis years.
Tithonus, the short-sighted, who
Forgot to ask against aging.
The fountain of youth. Its secret
Location via coded map.
The Ferris wheel, reversed, that spun
Adults to children in my cousin's
Comic book. His mother, months later,
Bringing a dove to his sickroom
Because the soul of the dying
So much loves the company of doves
It will linger. His transfusions.
His temporary color. His hands
Fluttering like flushed, frantic wings.

Holding the Babies

In old works of art, in the Madonna paintings,
Almost all of the Christ Childs are held on the left,
Teaching how mothers have always carried their young.

And when first we hold our own, supporting their heads
In astonishment and fear, who hasn't tucked them
To the left as if there's a better side for love?

Just anecdotal, but even the left-handed,
Carry their children this way, freeing the weak hand
For the minor work of gestures. And look, even

Young girls choose the left side for dolls, instinct we love
As much as the inherited explanation
For our handedness, how newborns are more at ease

With heartbeats than silence, how babies, from the left,
Hear better the reassurance of pulse, the way
Comfort must come from this, continuing the womb.

Science tests, these days, the theory of hemispheres,
How the right side of the brain gauges emotion,
Taking its cues for distress from the left, but when

They cannot prove the origin of our habit,
We are ecstatic with one mystery sustained,
Bonding with our newborns by the unknowable

Nature of ourselves, what we are and will become
Held in that natural pose, staring left and down
Along the absolute direction for delight.

The Invention of Prophecy

History was a test
so much of it wilderness
where madness begins.
Each week, another sign:
Hitler, then Israel, then

the collective antichrist
of Communist nations.
We could see for ourselves
in the repeated tests
of the A-bomb, the fallout
shelters of nonbelievers
who worshipped canned goods,
bottled water, and crackling,
one-station radios.
In the last days, they were
fools for permanence.
In the winter, their tracks
led to their yards' heavy doors.
My father said they'd started
the Scott Expedition
for the soul, that we'd been
waiting thousands of years
for the extraordinary light,
and now we were the lucky
living in the siren days,
the era of the wish-come-true.

The Fear Workshop

Write the man who can't manage a bridge. Have him
Believe he will suddenly swerve through the railing
And tumble his car into the dark, distant water.

Write a woman who avoids tunnels. Let her drive
Twenty miles instead of two. Describe her search
For a job in the states with the most level land.

Write the man who fears crossing streets. Watch him stop
At every curb because he cannot cross alone.
Make him follow the next crosser, close as a child.
Have him expect to stumble and feel his heart explode
In the crosswalk, his hands fluttering at his chest.

Write the man who can't live above the seventh floor.
Be certain he knows exactly how fast he'll fall,
Floor by floor, when he pitches through a window.
Let him learn the workings of elevators,
The history of their disasters, the strain
The safe stairs put upon the heart. Forget the fear
Of high-rise fires. This man waits for low-flying planes.

Write the woman, driving, who is afraid of bumps.
Have each jolt, by size, become a squirrel,
A rabbit, a deer. Make her stop and search
The woods for animals she is sure she's wounded.
Listen to her confess she's hit a hiker
On the highway. That she's checked under her car
For the maimed. Before you finish, walk outside
And lay your hands to the asphalt. Know what it is
To kneel on a road, traffic passing, to look
For bodies snared on an axle. Examine
The landscape. Everything is a body:
Bags, bushes, a bundle of misshapen wire.
Use your fingertips, your lips, your tongue.
Go ahead. Be deliberate. Make us believe it.

Voice Box

A woman on television

demonstrating the art of *qi gong*,
talking through the voice box
of her stomach. My father,
afterwards, saying, "She should
use the voice box God gave her."
My laryngitis from the dry heat
of the school where I teach.
My daughter, twenty-six, clearing
her throat each morning for
her smoke-stained voice, not yet
my uncle, at thirty, hoarse
and coughing until his voice box
was removed. His relearning
to talk, holding his electro-larynx
to his throat. The minister with
Lou Gehrig's disease pecking
out messages with a stick held
in his teeth. His wife showing us
his bound sermons. His tapping *yes*
or *no* to those he wishes her to read.
The birthday gifts my mother
wrapped six months in advance,
how they've sat, since her death,
twenty years gagged in her unused room,
waiting for their turn to speak.

Subsidence

It's not the atomic bomb, subsidence.
It's not the end of the world, the shifting
Of foundations, the cinderblock cracked where

Corners of houses keel over like drunks.
It's not fallout, the despair that covers
Homeowners in the helpless housing plan
Built over the long-closed, anthracite mines.
It's not a firestorm that ruins these roads,
Not a shock-wave that creates refugees.

It's not my father inside the fire hall
Huddled with his neighbors. It's not his hands
That straighten the map where his modest street
Shows so large he believes it's a river.

It's not cancer in every family.
It's not decades of dying, nobody
Returning, not ever, not even to
The half-life that they endured, measuring
Themselves by mortgages that outlive them.
It's not the apocalypse. It's not news,
Watching while my father walks his hallway,
Measuring slope with his body, leaning
Toward collapse like a crowd of widows.

The History of Permanence

One of the saints, his coffin reopened
By descendants of the faithful, had not
Decomposed. Blessed are the pure in heart,
They said, and even if the rest of us
Believe nothing of the Catholic ways,
What about those mummies who stayed and stayed,
No matter the lives they'd earlier lived?

Didn't those kings and queens still look themselves?
The ancient secrets of embalming said
We didn't have to turn to dust. And for
Those among us with little faith, there were
Mummy medicines, the dead-for-eons
Powdered to preserve them, and that failing,
The dust of those mummies mixed in with paint
To make art, at least, eternal. Look there,
In the detailed, brushstroked shades, something saved
For a thousand years, more than enough to
Outlast a world prophesized soon-to-die.
Those paintings would be juried, at last, to
The left- or right-hand halls of judgment, hung
In the permanent collection of God.

The Cabinet of Wonders

*Frederick Ruysch, the great embalmer, could fill
all the veins and arteries, none ruptured, before
his solution hardened* – from *FINDERS KEEPERS*

So expert, finally, at perfecting
Preservation, Ruysch worked with capillaries,
With filling the fine vessels of the face
So well these infants' heads in bottles float
Eyes open. As if surface still mattered.
Here, in this jar, an arm rising from lace
To grip an eye socket centuries old.

Here, a skull vented for a view of the brain.

Here, the small skeleton that holds a mayfly
To remind us of transience these mornings
When the *wunderkammer* of sickness takes
All the available space with the keepsakes
Of pain, the curios for fever, and
The repeated mementoes of wheezing.

In this museum in which we love ourselves,
The dispassionate fetus will not break
Its stare. Severed at the neck, we know, yet
Ruysch's daughter sewed the lace for its throat,
Selected beads, and sometimes she helped him clothe
His allegorical tableaux, fetal
Skeletons walking and weeping and playing
The violin with a dried-artery bow.

Look, I've listened to "possible mass" after one
Of those landscape kidney stones doubled me
Down to emergency. I've posed for
Tableaux With CAT-Scan and seen myself exposed
On the bulletin board for death, so many
Patients waiting in those subdivided rooms
We could have formed our own tableaux for fear,
A full *kunstkammer* where the conditions
Of our bodies could have been curated
To display the memory absolutions.

Whatever Ruysch is saying now, these rooms are
Weaving me inside. In the hypothesis
Of the Stendahl Syndriome, some tourists grow
Giddy after art. Their pulse accelerates.
They sweat and faint, or hallucinate, some

Of them depressed, some euphoric, some
Omnipotent in their hearts, though so many
Of these displays have been lost I can only
Trace the outline of every suspect organ
I can locate, running my fingers along
The perimeter of the liver to feel
For exactly what I want never to find.
Although as soon as I think this, I say
Of course not, how silly, like the doctor
Who, when I insisted I could distinguish
One kidney heavier than the other,
Shook his head sadly and said "impossible."

The Open Heart

In disaster movies, someone
Is always laid out for surgery,
Chest opened, when the earthquake strikes
Or the hurricane hits. Things blacken
Until the emergency lights
Come on, a generator running
Not quite strong enough to keep bulbs
From blinking, the room from turning hot.

As soon as the second plane struck,
The brief idea of accident
Exploding into fear, I tried
To mark how many of those patients.
Survived surgery while the world
Was changing because someone I knew
Was having his constricted heart

Paused, just then, for delicate repair.

We murmured in the waiting room,
The language veering from curse to prayer,
All that morning, our attention
To the news flickered as if our hearts
Were blinking off as well, dimming
To the darkness of apprehension
Where the anaesthetized can hear
The saddened voices of their surgeons.

He was going to die or wake
An afterthought for everyone but
Those who loved him. All of the talk
On television sounded like what
I'd heard a hundred times: Wreckage
And triage, evacuation, rescue,
The baffled crowd of civilians
Enveloped by clouds of toxic dust.

The future was a chest scar. A blue cough.
The word suddenly sparkled like a stroke.

The Exact Likeness for Grief

Swinging a pitching wedge, my father lofts
Seven golf balls over my mother's grave.
To spare the grass, he hits from the shoulder,
Picking them clean from the thin lie of dirt.

It's fifty yards, I'm guessing, to the woods
Where all but one of seven disappear
In yardage he can manage, length to spare,
At eighty-eight, his knees beyond repair.

He limps to her grave site, his love an arc
That ends among trees. The flowers he's picked
Follow him in my hands; he turns the club
Upside down and uses it as a cane.

"Some day you'll know," my father says, meaning
His knees, and then again, "Some day you'll know,"
Meaning this time, the grave, this selection
Of flowers, orange ones I cannot name.

My father, the prophet, bends to the vase
Of wilted stems. My father, who's warned me,
"You'll see" a thousand times, lifts the fresh buds
From my hands, steadies himself on my arm.

My father, who was a maintenance man,
Sends the old stems to the woods in my hands,
Seats the flowers by height like a teacher
While I kick the short ball into the trees.

You Know

You Know
(a sequence)

Her Piece

The woman whose one daughter was buried
By her killer tells me she wants to talk
To someone who will write everything down.
She means "to say her piece" in the paper
Where my column is printed once a week,
But we stick in two minutes of silence
After she begins, "It's awful to bear."

I nod like I know what it is to have
A child found after eight months in the ground.
The four rooms she rents face a wall that keeps
The Susquehanna from flooding her street
And the seven blocks before the city
Slopes up to hillsides where the rich can build.
"Over there," she finally says, "you know,"

Meaning beyond that wall where her daughter
Has surfaced, and she passes a small set
Of photographs I shuffle through and hold,
Embarrassed to lay them down. On top is
Her daughter at twenty, taken, she says,
"Just the month before." Outside, I can read
"Thank You Wall," those words repeated in paint

After April's flood crested three inches
From the brink. "Beforehand is when you know,"
She says. "It doesn't take Thomas to touch
The grave," trusting a Bible tale with me,
Adding, "You study her now. Find the words,"
Watching me clutch those photographs as if
I was already hearing those faces, too.

The First Dark Glasses

The street lights are aspirin.
My wife talks about the queen
Who bearded herself before
Ceremonies, convincing
Her soldiers to obey.
The air between us rattles;
The night is footsteps.
Along this road a father
Has thrown his child in front
Of a truck. Now, the headlights
Are cigarettes in the mouths
Of prisoners. We know
The knees of those cars will buckle,
And we cross and recross,
Diminishing ourselves like waves.
The first dark glasses, I say,
Were worn by judges to hide
How they felt about evidence.
She places her hands on my back.
"Get ready," she says, lights coming
From both sides like testimony.

Girls

My wife begins with hiding in a ditch
As a child, pressing herself to the dirt
As if her seventh grade homeroom teacher
Was evaluating her bomb drill form.
The men in the truck joked about fresh meat
That turned their truck around. One of them said,
"She'll have a story to tell tomorrow"
While he pissed upon the shoulder, so close
She heard the hiss of contact just before
A quirk of traffic chased their lust away.
She says the man who bought our house confessed
To raping "his girls" in the small room where
Our daughter slept for six years. Where she screamed,
One night, undressing, at a face against
Her window, sending us outside to where
We found the painted cinderblock that man
Had left behind, inviting us to check
The garages of our neighbors for proof.

After we moved, for one year, we walked back
To that house, returning until we thought
We'd never lived there. That father, she says,
Raped each daughter earlier than the last.
For privacy, that bedroom had two doors
To lock. Surely, the mother would try one
Or take to her tiptoes at the window.
What kept those three girls from screaming? What keeps
Us from setting fire to our former rooms?

A Scenario of Accomplices

The day, in early November, he takes
His daughter to Niagara Falls, it snows,
And from out of the crowd of cold tourists
A woman bends to say "What a darling,"
And suddenly, "Want to see?" She swings her
Up until she's squealing and squirming high
With delight just before he steps forward,
Fearing at first this woman is the one
Who can throw a child over the railing,
And then, with conviction, she's the woman
Who will steal her, flee into the crowd where
A scenario of accomplices
Will pass his child like a relay baton
While she squats down to disappear among
Families, rising again in a coat
That covers the purple sweater he's marked.
When he rushes that woman, when he tears
His child from her arms as she walks, he learns
The tight grip of somebody sure of theft
Or safety, his daughter's cry of surprise
Or sudden pain, a stranger spinning to
Curse him with an expression of loathing
As if he is a soldier assigning
Her child to a boxcar, saying nothing
As the crowd swirls her behind him, yet he
Keeps moving, looking for men he is sure
Are nearby, seeing him or him or him
Retreating as he passes, his daughter
Saying "what?" and "water" while he hurries

Away until there are so few people
They could be walking their own upstate street
On this Saturday morning, watched only
By a neighbor, someone like me, who cuts
His grass among flurries to get it trimmed
For winter, who thinks his daughter is sick
From the way he carries her to the car,
Who imagines he sees emergency,
Something to remark to his busy wife
Who will look across the street for the rest
Of the day, straining to see his story,
Reading the trouble by gesture, whether
It can pass or is inconsolable.

Stories

My daughter says that three men, this year, have jerked
Themselves off while she walked near them in New York.
She names teachers who suggested sex, the way
They managed ambiguity to protect
Themselves from guilt or shame, and I name a few
Of my own, including the one I worked with
Who married a girl he fucked, keeping his job.
The one who photographed fourth graders and moved
To another school. The one who, for years, touched
Enough sixth graders to finally be fired.

We're getting ready to talk about the man,
This afternoon, who showed her his back yard, who
Asked her what fish did in winter, guiding her
Toward his shadowed pond, asking, at last, how long

I'd be gone from the house we were visiting.
And because he's not a memory, because
He's standing on his screened-in porch fifty feet
From us, we lower our voices when we start
To talk about the needs we keep to ourselves
Until some of us eagerly surrender.

The Murder Interview

She was riding on his shoulders,
The father says—she waved at me.

He's describing, for reporters,
The last time he saw his daughter.

Alive, that is. With her killer,
We've been told, just minutes from death.

The father returned to yard work.
The girl, we know, climbed down and held

That boy's hand like a small sister
Beginning a walk in the woods.

After that, it's speculation—
The boy fifteen, the girl, seven

And her body, found this morning,
Undressed and beaten and strangled.

The father remembered that boy
Helping with the search, calling her

By a nickname. He remembers
The way his daughter bounced, laughing—

Like on a carousel, he says,
Like she was at the school picnic

Out to the park, the bumper cars
And the tilt-a-whirl coming next.

He lights a cigarette, asks us
If we want to follow him back

Through that forest to make believe
With ourselves. Take hold of my hand,

He says. Try my fingers for size,
Then just you wait till we get there.

The day's bruise widens like the wish
For leaving, the humidity

Of denial staining our shirts.
The moist light seeps into the earth.

All of us remember the weight
Of our children through our shoulders,

And we hold our breath, listening
To the childish cry of darkness.

Specificity

Specificity

For Len Roberts

Cause of death unknown. Had never been fatally ill before.
Death Certificate, 1880s

Until I was twelve, *worn out*
and *God's will* were the reasons
my relatives died, my mother
speaking like a doctor, citing
visual evidence
or unknowable matters
of faith as if each were
a diagnosis of disease.

In the King James edition
of medicine, the self-help
my grandmother relied on,
there was the finality
of dropsy, the chronic palsies,
what Jesus cured, like leprosy
and possession, the devil
imbedded in the flesh like ticks.

Before she was born? People died
from convulsions and fever,
from infancy, age and tissick,
the collective name for killers
that came with coughs, as frequent
as smallpox and grip of the guts,

what the dying did, at last,
when their digestion failed.

Approximation. Guesswork.
Less of that now, the x-ray
showing the shadow that will kill us,
the blood sample spilling numbers
that count us out, each tremor
specific, a thousand names
exactly right, pinpointing
each particular way to die.

Amyloidosis, for instance,
how one friend, this week, has gone.
And now, after memorial,
after an hour of tributes
by poets who traveled hours
to eulogize, I sit with my wife
who orders a glass of Chambord
for a small, expensive pleasure

in a well-decorated room,
the possibility of happiness
surprising us in the way
hummingbirds do, stuck in the air,
just now, outside this window,
attracted to the joy of sweetness
despite the clear foreshadowing
of their tiny, sprinting hearts.

GARY FINCKE, through twelve books of poems published over twenty-four years, has built a reputation for his skill at combining the realism of personal narrative with the realism of the fantastic precisely imagined.

His poems have appeared frequently in nearly every well-regarded journal,
including *The Paris Review, Ploughshares*, the *Virginia Quarterly Review*, the *Missouri Review*, the *Kenyon Review*, the *Georgia Review*, and the *Gettysburg Review*. Reprinted in *Harper's*, the *Pushcart Prize* volumes, *Poetry Daily*, and *Verse Daily*, he has won the Ohio State University Press/The Journal Poetry Book Prize and the Bess Hokin Prize from *Poetry* magazine.

He is the Charles Degenstein Professor of Creative Writing at Susquehanna University, where he directs the Writers Institute.